Exciting Entertainers

Jen Green

920.02

Published by **Atebol Cyfyngedig**, Fagwyr Buildings, Llandre, Aberystwyth, Ceredigion, SY24 5AQ
01970 832 172
www.atebol.com
www.ateducationalbooks.com

ISBN: 978 1 909666 60 3

Project Managers: Dafydd Saunders Jones, Megan Elizabeth Tye
Editor: Gill Matthews
Design: Ceri Jones Studio, stiwdio@ceri-talybont.com
Picture Research: Dafydd Saunders Jones and Megan Elizabeth Tye
Published with the financial support of the Welsh Books Council
Printed by Cambrian Printers, Aberystwyth, Ceredigion

Photographs: Alamy Images, Getty Images, and Sir Tom Jones Private Collection (cover)
Alamy Images: pp 3, 4/5, 6/7, 10/11, 12/13, 14/15, 16/17, 18/19, 20/21, 22/23, 24/25, 28/29
Getty Images: pp 3, 4/5, 6/7, 8/9, 10/11, 12/13, 16/17, 18/19, 24/25, 26/27, 28/29
Sir Tom Jones Private Collection: pp 3, 4/5, 28/29
Shutterstock Images: 20/21

Acknowledgements
Atebol wishes to thank Jen Green for her professionalism during the preparation of these resources.
We would also wish to thank all the individuals included in this book for their support and enthusiasm during the development of this book.

Contents

In the spotlight   4

Actor: **Matthew Rhys**   6

Singer: **Katherine Jenkins**   8

Actor / comedian: **Rob Brydon**   10

Actress / screenwriter: **Ruth Jones**   12

Actor: **Rhys Ifans**   14

Harpist: **Catrin Finch**   16

Presenter: **Alex Jones**   18

Comedian: **Rhod Gilbert**   20

Screenwriter: **Russell T Davies**   22

Actress: **Eve Myles**   24

Commentator: **Jonathan Davies**   26

Singer: **Tom Jones**   28

Quiz: Are you cut out to be an entertainer?   30

Glossary   31

In the spotlight

Introduction

Welsh entertainers and musicians have topped the bill ever since singer Tom Jones and actor Anthony Hopkins rose to fame in the 1960s. This book highlights some of Wales' most talented artists, including actors, singers, musicians, writers and broadcasters. Find out how they got started, and about the highs and lows of fame.

Starting out in...

Performing arts

Welsh arts and performance date back at least to the 1170s, when the first eisteddfod was held in Cardigan. Fancy yourself as a budding actor? Theatr Clwyd (www.clwyd-theatr-cymru.co.uk/) has acting courses. Welsh stars such as Rob Brydon and Eve Myles trained at the Royal Welsh College of Music and Drama in Cardiff – see www.rwcmd.ac.uk/.

Music

Wales has a proud tradition of music and song. From classical performers such as Katherine Jenkins and harpist Catrin Finch through choirs to rock and pop stars, Welsh musicians excel at all kinds of music. Katherine Jenkins says: "My advice to young singers is to either join your school or church choir or find one in your local area." Think about applying to the Royal Welsh College of Music and Drama, or just form a band with your friends!

Comedy

Welsh performers have a strong flair for comedy, from Max Boyce to Rob Brydon and Rhod Gilbert. Most comedians start out in stand-up. Rob Brydon has this tip: "When you're doing stand-up, you can comment if something fails, get a laugh from that."

Writing and broadcasting

Welsh writers have written some of the most popular plays and TV shows of today, from *Under Milk Wood* to *Doctor Who* and sitcom smash *Gavin and Stacey*. Screenwriters, actors and broadcasters such as Ruth Jones and Alex Jones started out in radio or TV at BBC Wales and S4C.

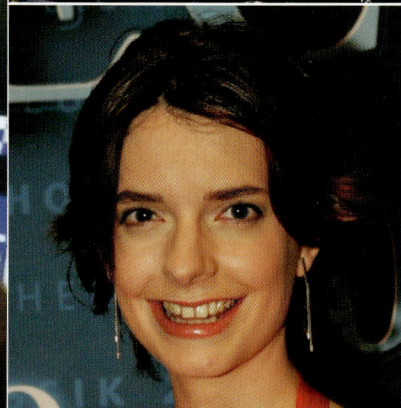

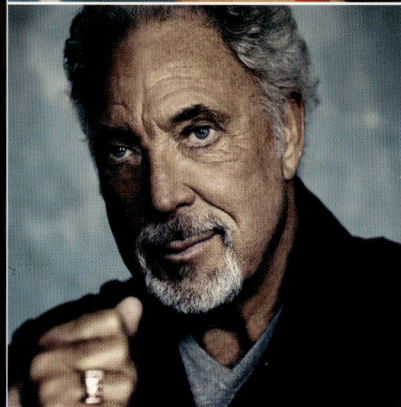

Do you really want to be an entertainer? Go to page 30 to find out!

Price of fame

Many people dream of being famous, but do you really want to be recognised everywhere you go? Presenter Alex Jones says: "People stop me and have a chat, wherever I am… the lovely thing is that they speak to you as if they know you very well." However actress Ruth Jones warns that people mistake her for the characters she plays. "I have to go, 'You know it's only pretend, don't you?'"

Matthew Rhys

Matthew Rhys's acting career has taken him a long way from Wales, to the United States and New Zealand. His roles include Dylan Thomas, Elvis Presley and a Russian spy.

Profile

Name:	Matthew Rhys Evans
Born:	8 November 1974 in Cardiff
Lives:	California

Did you know?

Matthew is good friends with Welsh actor Ioan Gruffudd, who also lives in California. They shared a house for almost ten years and Matthew was best man at Ioan's wedding. Of living so far away Matthew says: "There's such a unique humour in Wales that I love and miss."

"It's an actor's dream to play a wide variety of parts."

Honours board

Lawyer Kevin Walker, *Brothers and Sisters* ((2006 - 2011).
Poet Dylan Thomas, *The Edge of Love* (2008).
Spy Phillip Jennings in *The Americans* (2013).
Dashing Mr Darcy in *Death Comes to Pemberley* (2013).

In 2013 Matthew played Jane Austen heart-throb Mr Darcy in the BBC drama *Death Comes to Pemberley*.

Getting started

The son of two schoolteachers, Matthew went to two Welsh-language schools in Cardiff. After starring as Elvis Presley in a school musical he trained at the Royal Academy of Dramatic Art (RADA) in London. See www.rada.ac.uk/.

Big break

In 2005 Matthew landed a starring role in the US family drama *Brothers and Sisters* and moved to California. He played gay lawyer Kevin Walker. The show ran for five seasons until 2011.
"I got a lot out of *Brothers and Sisters* and learnt some incredible things."

Insider info

In 2013 Matthew played a Russian spy in *The Americans*. His character Phillip Jennings has spent 15 years pretending to be American, and has two children who know nothing of his real identity. The plot is based on the true story of Russian sleeper agents who spent years living undercover in the US.

Prep

Preparing for his role as undercover agent involved doing martial arts training. On holiday in Mongolia, Matthew tried to put his new skills into practice when challenged to a wrestling contest. The result was a painful shoulder injury.

Katherine Jenkins

"Singing has always been my big passion."

Pop, opera, show tunes, hymns – diva Katherine Jenkins sings them all. The fastest selling mezzo-soprano ever, her nine albums have sold all over the world.

Did you know?

Katherine once shattered a chandelier with her top note. "There was this massive bang and all this glass came down from the ceiling. I'd like that to be my party trick if I can perfect it."

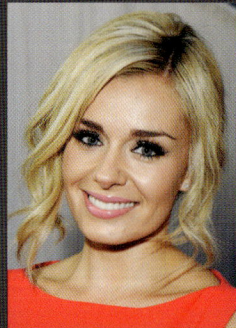

Profile

Name:	Katherine Jenkins
Born:	29 June 1980 in Neath
Lives:	London
Career:	As a choirgirl Katherine won several singing competitions. She became famous after performing at Westminster Cathedral in London in 2003.

Getting started

Katherine studied at the Royal Academy of Music in London: see www.ram.ac.uk/. She has also been a model, and was the Face of Wales 2000. She has worked as a tour guide on the London Eye!

Insider info

Katherine sings mezzo-soprano – a little lower than the highest female voice, soprano, but higher than the lower voice, alto. As a "crossover artist", she sings many different musical styles.

Big break

In 2007 her fifth album, *Rejoice,* entered the pop charts at number three, above the Spice Girls and Girls Aloud. Katherine commented: "I never imagined that I would outsell the Spice Girls and Celine Dion."

TV credits

Katherine's many TV appearances include being a guest on the *X Factor* final in 2007. Her first acting role was in the Christmas special of *Doctor Who* in 2010. In 2012 she came second in the American celebrity ballroom dancing show, *Dancing with the Stars*.

Charity run

In 2013 Katherine ran the London Marathon, crossing the finishing line in five hours 26 minutes. Her run raised £25,000 for the cancer charity Macmillan. She dedicated her run to her father, Selwyn, who died of lung cancer at the age of 70 when she was 15.

Under fire

Katherine has visited war zones several times to entertain British troops. In 2005 in Iraq the helicopter she was travelling in was fired on by a missile. "There was this incredibly loud noise and the helicopter just dropped out of the sky. Somehow the pilot landed and we were pulled out."

Rob Brydon

Welsh actor Rob Brydon is one of Britain's best-known comedians. He presents the BBC TV show *Would I Lie to You?* and is also a scriptwriter, singer and impressionist.

"If you're a comedian, you are looking for material in daily life."

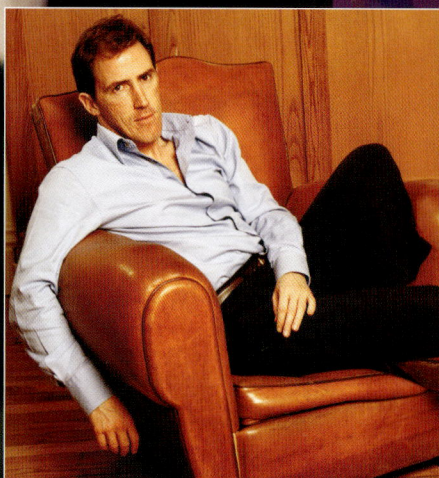

Did you know?

Rob also went to school with glamorous filmstar Catherine Zeta-Jones, and once stole her lunch money.

Profile

Name:	Robert Brydon Jones
Born:	3 May 1965 in Swansea
Lives:	Richmond, London, with his wife Claire and sons Tom and George

Getting started

Rob went to the Royal Welsh College of Music and Drama but left after a year to join BBC Radio Wales. He stayed there for six years as a DJ and presenter, and also worked on TV.

Big break

In 2000 Rob starred in the BBC black comedy *Human Remains* (2000) with Julia Davis. In six programmes he and Julia played six different couples. The series with its deadpan style was unusual and really got Rob noticed.

TV greatest hits

Rob's best known TV shows include *Marion and Geoff* (2000 and 2003), which he co-wrote… and starred in as the innocent Keith Barret. He starred as Uncle Bryn in the smash BBC sitcom *Gavin and Stacey* (2007 - 2010). He has regularly appeared as a parody of himself with fellow comedian Steve Coogan.

Insider info

Rob is a brilliant impressionist. His impressions include singer Tom Jones, comedian Ronnie Corbett and actors Roger Moore and Richard Burton. But the best impression of all is his famous "Small Man in a Box".

Did you know?

Rob first met Ruth Jones, co-star of *Gavin and Stacey,* at school in Swansea.

Number One

Rob is a talented singer. In 2009 his version of "Islands in the stream" with Gavin and Stacey co-star Ruth Jones and singers Tom Jones and Robin Gibb got to number one! The song raised £5.5 million for Comic Relief.

Honours board

The shows *Human Remains* and *Marion and Geoff* both won British Comedy Awards. In 2013 Rob was awarded the MBE for his services to comedy, broadcasting and also to charity.

Ruth Jones

Ruth Jones is a rare thing in entertainment: an actress who is also a writer and TV producer. The star of *Stella* and *Gavin and Stacey* is a familiar face on TV, but says she still hasn't got to grips with the "fame thing".

Did you know?

Ruth went to the same school in Porthcawl as comedian Rob Brydon. Ruth and Rob starred in the hit sitcom *Gavin and Stacey*, which Ruth co-wrote with James Corden, who also starred in *Fat Friends*.

Profile

Name:	Ruth Alexandra Elizabeth Jones
Born:	22 September 1966 in Bridgend, south Wales
Lives:	Cardiff with her husband, David Peet, with whom she started the production company Tidy. She has three grown-up stepchildren

Getting started

After leaving school Ruth went to Warwick University to study English and Theatre. After graduating from Warwick she went to the Royal Welsh College of Music and Drama in Cardiff. See www.rwcmd.ac.uk/.

Big break

Ruth found it hard to get acting work at first. But after working for BBC Wales she landed roles with the Royal Shakespeare Company and The National Theatre. A role in the hit movie *East is East* was followed by a part in the ITV comedy *Fat Friends,* which ran for four series (2000 - 2005).

Honours board

Myfanwy in *Little Britain* (2003-6)
Asthmatic assistant Linda in the black comedy *Nighty Night* (2004/05)
Comedian Hattie Jacques in *Hattie* (2011).
Ruth currently stars as Stella in the Sky One comedy drama *Stella*, which is set in the Welsh valleys. The series is produced by Ruth and husband David's TV company, Tidy.

"My life in seven words... packed, funny, blessed, happy and highly unpredictable."

Insider info

The BBC hit comedy *Gavin and Stacey* was about the romance between Gavin from Essex and Stacey from the Vale of Glamorgan in Wales. Ruth and co-writer James Corden also starred as Nessa and Smithy. Ruth says: "The show does generate a lot of warmth. People seem to like that, especially when things aren't terribly jolly." The show ran for four years from 2007 to 2010.

Rhys Ifans

The tall, lanky actor can turn his hand to any role, from romantic lead to slob, gambler and a three-metre-tall green monster.

"If it is not scary, it is not worth doing."

Did you know?

Rhys's first love was rock music. He was lead singer in Welsh rock band Super Furry Animals before they became famous. He still sings, with psychedelic rock band The Peth, along with Dafydd Ieuan from Super Furry Animals. Peth is Welsh for Thing.

Profile

Name:	Rhys Owain Evans
Born:	22 July 1967 in Haverfordwest, Pembrokeshire
Career:	Welsh TV and stage actor before moving into Hollywood movies

Honours board

Loveable slob Spike in *Notting Hill* (1999)
Dangerously unhinged Jed Parry in *Enduring Love* (2004)
Xenophilius Lovegood in *Harry Potter and the Deathly Hallows: Part 1* (2010)
Villainous Dr Curt Connors / The Lizard in *The Amazing Spider-Man* (2012)

Big break

Rhys took acting classes at Theatr Clwyd in Mold while at school. Check out Theatr Clwyd on www.clwyd-theatr-cymru.co.uk/. He then trained at the Guildhall School of Music and Drama in London. His big break came in 1997 when he starred with his brother Llŷr in the Swansea-based film *Twin Town*. The brothers played twins.

Prep

Rhys prepared for his role as slovenly Spike in *Notting Hill* by not washing or brushing his teeth! He stole the show from his glamorous co-stars Hugh Grant and Julia Roberts, and was nominated for a BAFTA award for Best Actor in a Supporting Role.

Insider Info

State-of-the-art computer graphics transformed Rhys into a three-metre-tall green lizard for *The Amazing Spider-Man*. "I had a green suit on, and then this cardboard head, and these big claws… The technology is so advanced now that when the Lizard's eyes move, they're my eyes. If I frown or show any emotion, they're my emotions."

Catrin Finch

> "My aim is to popularise the harp as an instrument. It is quite unknown really."

Insider info: About the harp

The harp is the national instrument of Wales. The modern concert harp has 47 strings. There are seven pedals, which change the notes played. The instrument stands about 1.85 metres (6 ft 1 in) tall and weighs 36 kg (80 lbs).

Catrin is a woman with a mission! Her aim is to make the harp better known and more popular. She has made her own arrangements of classic pieces so they can be played on the harp.

Profile

Name:	Catrin Anna Finch
Born:	1980 in Llan-non, Ceredigion
Lives:	Cardiff, where she runs a recording studio with her husband, Hywel Wigley, a sound engineer. The couple have two daughters, Ana Gwen and Pegi.

Harpist Catrin Finch is used to rubbing shoulders with royalty. In 2000 she was appointed official harpist to the Prince of Wales – a post that had not been filled since the time of Queen Victoria!

Did you know?

Catrin's first harp teacher, Elinor Bennett, is now her mother-in-law. She and Elinor's son Hywel Wigley got married in 2003.

Wonderkid

Catrin took up the harp at the age of six. At nine she received the highest mark ever given in the UK for harp grade 8 exam. At ten she joined the National Youth Orchestra of Great Britain – see www.nyo.org.uk/. She became the orchestra's youngest member to play at the Proms concerts in London.

Getting started

From 7 to 16 Catrin had harp lessons from expert harpist Elinor Bennett. Later she studied at Purcell School, a special music school, and at the Royal Academy of Music in London.

Big break

In 2000 at the age of 20, Catrin shot to fame after being appointed royal harpist. The post had not been filled since 1873! The job gave her the chance to play in royal palaces all over the world.

Honours board

In 2003 Catrin presented a TV documentary about her job as royal harpist called *Charlie's Angel*. It won a BAFTA/Cymru award as best music programme. Her performance of *Palladio* by Welsh composer Karl Jenkins has had nearly a million hits on YouTube. Her harp recordings are sold all over the world.

Alex Jones

"My job is amazing. I really don't think there is a nicer show to be on."

In 2010 Alex Jones landed her dream job – presenting the BBC's early-evening magazine programme *The One Show*. A fluent Welsh speaker, she also presents programmes on the Welsh-language channel S4C.

Strictly Come Dancing

In 2011 Alex took part in *Strictly Come Dancing*. She and partner James Jordan got as far as the semi-finals. Alex says: "It was one of the best times of my life."

Profile

Name:	Charlotte Alexandra Jones
Born:	18 March 1977 in Ammanford, Carmarthenshire
Lives:	London

Getting started

Alex went to Maes yr Yrfa Welsh-language school in Llanelli. As a girl she trained as a ballet dancer. She went on to study theatre, film and television at Aberystwyth University – see www.aber.ac.uk/en/tfts/.

Big break

After university Alex began working as a TV researcher before trying out as a presenter. Her first presenting job was on the Welsh-language programme *Cân i Gymru* (*A Song for Wales*). She went on to present the travel show *Tocyn* (*Ticket*) and the extreme sports show *Chwa* on S4C. In August 2010 she landed the job on *The One Show*. Other TV credits include hosting *Let's Dance for Comic Relief*.

The One Show

Working on *The One Show* has taken Alex to many parts of the world and involved all sorts of experiences. Some, but not all, have been glamorous! As part of the *Grin and Bear It* challenge she cleaned drains under London! She has also danced at Buckingham Palace with co-presenter Matt Baker.

Insider info

Alex's job on *The One Show* involves interviewing celebrities for four minutes. The challenge is "trying to build a relationship with that person on screen, and trying to explain and steer them through the show, whilst you're live on air".

Rhod Gilbert

"In the Bible, God made it rain for 40 days and 40 nights. That's a pretty good summer for Wales. That's a hosepipe ban waiting to happen. I was eight before I realised you could take a cagoule off."

Big break

Rhod only started in comedy at the age of 34, after being "constantly nagged" by his girlfriend, who thought he was funny. He took part in the Edinburgh Festival Fringe in 2005. This is an international arts festival specialising in comedy. Rhod was an instant hit, and has performed at the Edinburgh Fringe every year since.

Profile

Name:	Rhodri Paul Gilbert
Born:	18 October 1968 in Carmarthen
Lives:	Claims to live in the imaginary village of Llanbobl but in fact lives in Cardiff

Getting started

Rhod was a telly-addict as a boy. He went to Exeter University to study languages, but was painfully shy at first. After university he travelled in Asia and Australia before working first for the Welsh Office and then as a market researcher.

Stand-up comic Rhod Gilbert is one of Britain's funniest comedians. His quirky stories and fast-paced delivery make him a brilliant live performer.

"I was in school in the 1970's. A jam sandwich was considered two of your five a day..."

Did you know?

Many of Rhod's stories are about life in the village of Llanbobl where he says he lives. Llanbobl doesn't exist, but after his shows, many people tell him they have been there for their holidays!

Honours board

The BBC TV panel show *Ask Rhod Gilbert* (2010/11)
Rhod Gilbert's Bulging Barrel of Laughs, Radio 2 (2010)
Rhod's story about a lost suitcase has had more than seven million hits on YouTube.
Rhod appears regularly on the TV comedy shows *Have I Got News for You?*, *Never Mind the Buzzcocks* and *Would I lie to You?*.

Rhod has hosted a regular Saturday morning show for BBC Radio Wales since 2007.

Insider info

In the TV series *Rhod Gilbert's Work Experience* Rhod tries out all sorts of jobs, from binman and butler to soldier, hairdresser and ordinary mother. "Being a mum was just as hard a slog as being a binman, even harder I reckon, and just as smelly."

Russell T Davies

"*Doctor Who* is bigger than any actor... I love them all."

TV producer and screenwriter Russell T Davies was the writer behind the incredibly successful relaunch of the TV science fiction series *Doctor Who*. He also wrote the *Doctor Who* spin-off series *Torchwood* and *The Sarah Jane Adventures*.

"It's exciting when you get kids in the playground talking about your story, because that's interactive television, that's what it's all about."

Profile

Name:	Stephen Russell Davies
Born:	27 April 1963 in Swansea
Lives:	Manchester

Getting started

Russell grew up in the 1960s in a family that "never switched the TV off". *Doctor Who* was his favourite programme. As a boy he wanted to be a comic-book artist, but a career advisor said this would be difficult, as he is colour-blind. He studied English Literature at Oxford University, before joining the BBC children's department as a script-writer and producer. He then moved on to write adult TV drama.

Big break

In 2003 the BBC decided to bring back *Doctor Who*, which had run from 1963 to 1989, but had not been on air since. Russell was approached by the BBC to write the new series and he decided he wanted a new kind of Doctor, someone who was "your best friend; someone you want to be with all the time". He decided to avoid the Doctor's past history and the Time Lords, but keep his spaceship, the TARDIS, and the Daleks. The new series, broadcast in 2005, was an international smash hit and is still running.

Honours board

In 2009 Russell quit *Doctor Who*. His adult spin-off, *Torchwood*, ran from 2006 to 2011, children's series *The Sarah Jane Adventures* from 2007 to 2011. His latest science fantasy drama for teens is *Wizards vs Aliens*.

Insider info

Doctor Who is the world's longest-running science fiction TV series. To date there have been 798 episodes, of which 106 are missing. Twelve actors have played the Doctor so far, from William Hartnell (1963-66) to Peter Capaldi (2013 onwards).

Eve Myles

Actress Eve Myles is best known for her role as Gwen Cooper in the *Doctor Who* sci-fi spin-off *Torchwood*. Her career has taken her from Powys to London, Hollywood and back again.

"Whether it be sci-fi, whether it be Shakespeare, you try and do it to the best of your ability."

Did you know?

Eve's *Torchwood* character Gwen Cooper is used to fighting aliens. In real life, Eve grew up in a family that loved boxing. She tried the sport herself but gave up after breaking her knuckles on a punchbag.

Profile

Name:	Eve Myles
Born:	26 July 1978 in Ystradgynlais, Powys
Lives:	with husband Bradley Freegard and daughter Matilda in Hollywood, USA, or wherever her work takes her!

Big break

In 2000 Eve landed the star role of Ceri Owen in the BBC Wales drama *Belonging*. The show ran until 2009 – Eve's longest acting part. She also did a spell with the Royal Shakespeare Company and at the National Theatre in London.

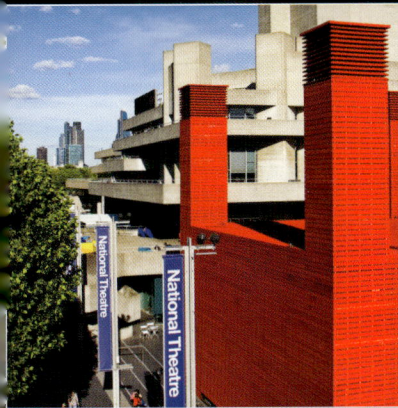

Insider info

Eve went to Ysgol Maesydderwen in Swansea and then studied acting at the Royal Welsh College of Music and Drama. She graduated in 2000.

Even bigger break!

A small role in a *Doctor Who* episode in 2005 got her noticed by *Doctor Who* producer and writer Russell T Davies. Davies called her "one of Wales' best kept secrets". When Davies got the go-ahead to write *Torchwood* he wrote the part of Gwen Cooper especially for her.

Eve says getting the part of Gwen Cooper written for her was like getting "my own personal Oscar". Gwen is level-headed but tough. "She's a social worker who can run and fight and stand in her own corner and win." Set in Cardiff, *Torchwood* ran for four series, from 2006 to 2011, and might be back one day.

Key roles

Lady Helen of Mora and witch Mary Collins in the BBC fantasy drama *Merlin* (2008).
Businesswoman, wife and mother Ceri Owen (Lewis) in the BBC Wales drama *Belonging* (2000 - 2009).
Plucky Gwen Cooper in *Torchwood* (2006 - 2011).
Dedicated district nurse Frankie in the BBC drama *Frankie* (2013).

Honours board

In 2007 Eve won a BAFTA Cymru for her role as Gwen Cooper in *Torchwood*. She has been nominated for the award five more times, including in 2002, 2003 and 2009 for her part as Ceri Owen, and also in 2008 and 2010 for other acting parts.

Jonathan Davies

What Jonathan Davies doesn't know about rugby isn't worth knowing! The sports expert is a former rugby union and rugby league star.

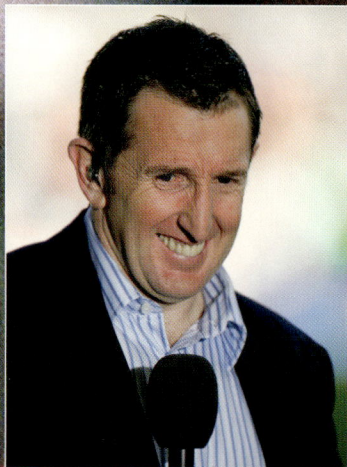

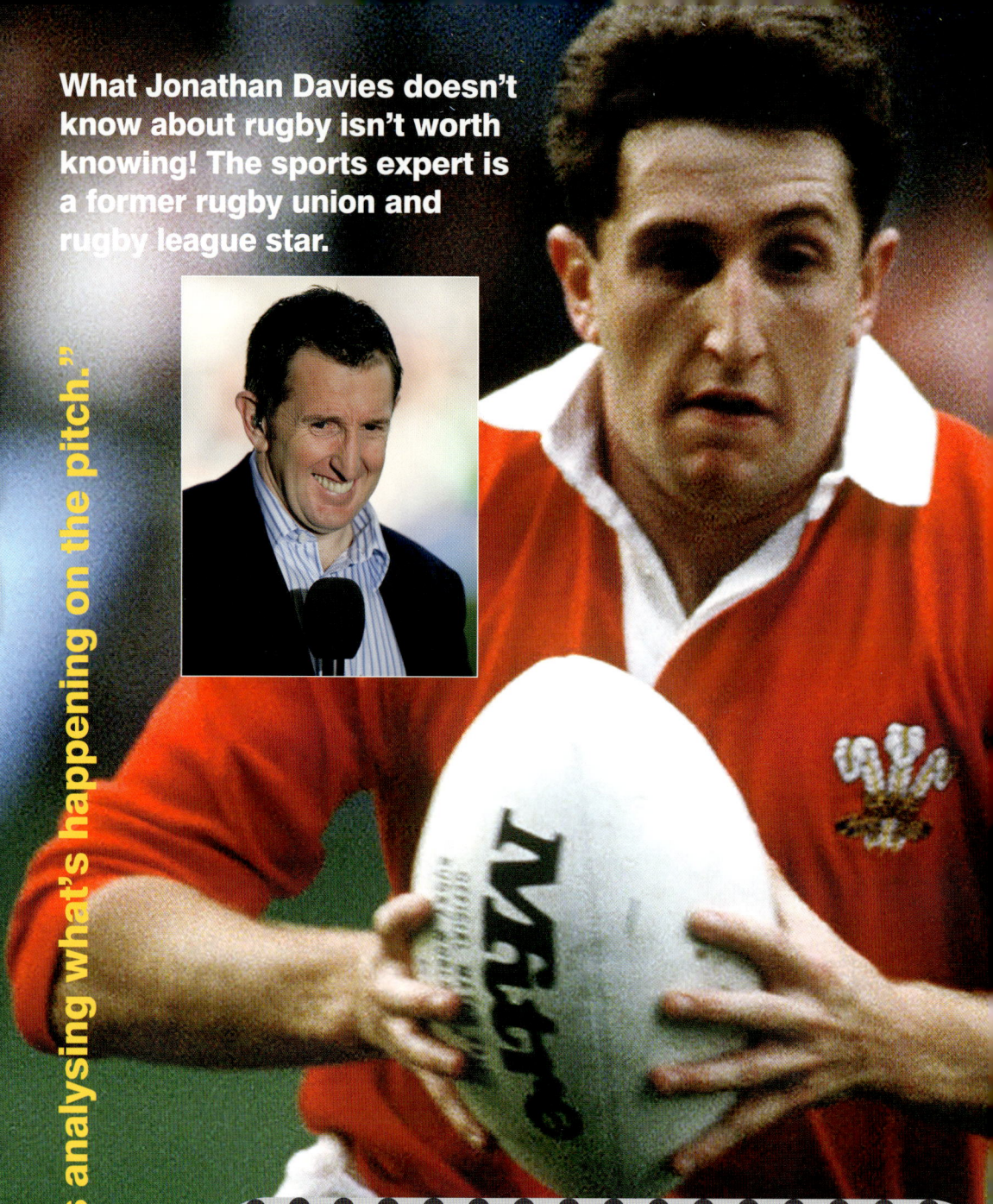

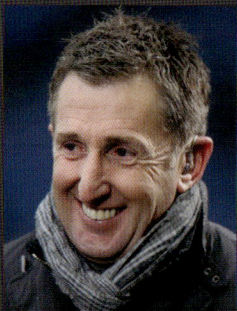

"My job is analysing what's happening on the pitch."

Profile

Name:	Jonathan D Davies, known as "Jiffy"
Born:	24 October 1962 in Trimsaran, Carmarthenshire
Career:	Jonathan has had three successful careers – as a rugby union international, a rugby league star and then sports commentator.

Starting out – rugby union

At school Jonathan showed great flair for rugby. He began in rugby union, and was signed by Neath RFC in 1982. In his first match for Wales he scored a try and a drop goal and was made man of the match. From 1985 to 1997 he represented Wales in 32 rugby union matches. After captaining Neath he moved to Llanelli RFC.

Move to rugby league – and back again

1988 brought a bold move. Jonathan moved to rugby league side Widnes in Cheshire for a record sum. He helped Widnes to win the World Cup Challenge before moving to their rivals Warrington in 1993. In the seven years he played rugby league he played for Wales many times. But after a short spell in Australia he switched back to rugby union, signing with Cardiff RFC in 1995.

Insider info: League vs Union?

Both rugby union and rugby league developed from rugby football. So what's the difference? Rugby union is traditionally played in the south of Britain, rugby league in the north. The two split in 1895, when northern clubs broke away to allow players to receive money for wages lost playing rugby. Northern league clubs soon allowed players to turn pro. The rules are also different. Rugby union has 15 players, league 13. In rugby league a player stands up and nudges the ball back after being tackled. In rugby union they ruck over the ball and carry on with the game. Rugby union finally went pro in 1995.

Family man

In 1983 Jonathan married Karen Hopkins, whom he had met at school aged 11. They had three children, Scott, Grace and Geena. But soon after Geena was born Karen discovered she had cancer. She died in 1997, leaving Jonathan to raise his family. He married his second wife, Helen, in 2002.

Sports commentator

Since retiring from professional sport Jonathan has worked as a sports commentator, for both rugby union and rugby league. He covers matches in both Welsh and English, and hosts his own chat show on S4C in Welsh.

Sir Tom Jones

"The fire is still in me. Not to be an oldie, but a goodie. I want to be a contender."

Sir Tom Jones has been in the music business for half a century! Still cool, the singer released his first record in 1964. Since 2012, his appearance on the BBC talent show *The Voice UK* has won him new fans.

Profile

Name:	Thomas John Woodward
Born:	7 June 1940 in Treforest, Pontypridd, Glamorgan
Lives:	Los Angeles, USA, since 1974, but often visits Britain

Tom sings all kinds of pop music: rock, country, blues, soul, gospel… He has sold over 100 million records and had an amazing 36 Top 40 hits in the UK, and 19 in the USA.

Early years

Tom's father, Thomas, was a coal miner. Tom began singing as a boy. In 1957, aged just 16, he married his high school sweetheart Melinda, who was also 16. Their son Mark was born soon after. Tom worked in a glove factory and in the building trade to support his wife and son. Tom and Melinda are still together.

Big break

In 1963 Tom joined a beat group, *Tommy Scott and the Senators.* A manager named Gordon Mills spotted his singing talent, took him to London, and got him a contract with Decca record company. He had his first hits between 1965 and 1967 with 'It's Not Unusual', 'What's New Pussycat?' and 'Green, Green Grass of Home'.

Later career

From the late 1960s to the early 80s Tom starred in his own TV shows in the UK and America. More hits followed in the 1970s, 80s and 90s and 2000s. He continues to have a very active recording and touring career, and in 2012 his role as coach on *The Voice UK* introduced him to a new generation of fans.

Inspiration

Tom owes his bluesy style to American soul music. In his teens, he was also a big fan of Elvis Presley, who later became a good friend.

Honours board

'What's New Pussycat?' won him the Grammy Award for Best New Artist, in 1966. Many other music awards followed. In 1999 he was awarded the OBE for his services to music. In 2006 he was given a knighthood, and became Sir Tom.

Quiz

Are you cut out to be an entertainer?

Have you got what it takes to get to the very top in entertainment? Find out by taking this quiz.

1. Every star performer must have star quality. Have you got the talent to shine?

    a. If I'm honest, my talents are about average in my chosen field.

    b. I'm lucky – I do have plenty of natural ability at what I love doing.

    c. I'm pretty good at what I do but I am not the best.

2. Do you hunger after fame or are you a shrinking violet?

    a. I'm pretty shy and hate being the focus of attention.

    b. I love being the centre of attention and long to see my name in lights!

    c. I don't mind being in the spotlight but not all the time.

3. To make it to the top you need steely determination and maybe a streak of ruthlessness.

    a. I believe everyone should have their chance to shine.

    b. I don't let anything stand in the way of my dream.

    c. I like to come first but am willing to let others take their turn at the top.

4. To give your best performance day in, day out, you need stamina. What's your staying power like?

    a. I have to admit I get discouraged quite quickly if things don't go my way.

    b. I stick at things to achieve my goal. My motto is "If at first you don't succeed, try, try again".

    c. I give it a go but I don't believe in "flogging a dead horse".

Results

Mostly a: You don't seem cut out to be a star at the moment, but perhaps you just haven't found the area in which you shine.

Mostly b: You've got what it takes to be a star: talent, ego, determination and staying power. Go for your dream!

Mostly c: You may have the talent, but at present you lack the drive to be a star.

Glossary

Celebrity	someone who is famous.
Contender	someone who takes part in a contest or struggles against difficulties.
Co-star	one of two or more famous actors who appear in the same film or programme.
Co-writer	one of two or more writers who work together on a piece of writing.
Crossover artist	a performer who performs different styles.
Deadpan	when an actor delivers his or her lines in a matter-of-fact way, without emotion.
Diva	a glamorous female performer, such as an opera singer.
Eisteddfod	a Welsh annual festival of literature, music and performance.
Excel	to do better than others at something.
Generation	a group of people all born around the same time.
Graduate	when a student finishes his or her course, and gets a degree or diploma.
Magazine programme	a TV programme that presents a number of topics, and usually includes interviews.
Market researcher	someone who gathers information about consumer choices – what people like to buy.
Mezzo-soprano	the female voice between the high voice, soprano, and the lower voice, alto; also a singer who sings in this range.
Popularise	to make something more popular.
Producer	the person who controls the production and financing of a film, play or TV programme.
Screenwriter	a writer who writes scripts for films or TV programmes – work that will be shown on screen.
Sitcom	short for situation comedy: a comedy based around certain characters in a given situation, such as a family or workplace.
Sleeper agent	a spy who spends years undercover.
Sound engineer	someone who works in a recording studio and controls the balance of music and other sounds.
The Proms	a summer season of daily classical music concerts, held in London.
Vinyl	a resin or plastic which was traditionally used to make records, before CDs were invented.